Blueprints of Twin Flames

The Awaking of the New Era

Grace Brewster

This book was written through lived experience, reflection, and remembrance.

Its words may be quoted, shared, or referenced only with respect for the work and its source. No part of this book may be reproduced or distributed in full without written permission from the author.

What follows is not doctrine, instruction, or promise. It is an invitation, a perspective shaped by consciousness observing itself through a human life. Any people, places, or moments described are filtered through personal experience and perception.

This book does not claim authority over truth. It offers resonance.

Readers are invited to engage with the material in a way that honors their own discernment, autonomy, and inner knowing.

First Edition: 2026
ISBN: 978-1-0698494-8-9
Self Published

Acknowledgments

To the Consciousness of the Blueprint: Thank you for the vision, the geometry, and the persistent nudge to put these frequencies into words. Thank you for choosing me to hold the pen and for trusting me to anchor these truths into the physical world.

To the Source: For the "High Voltage" that guides us and the "Divine Buffer" that protects us. Thank you for the reminder that we are never truly separate from the light or from each other.

To the Catalyst: For being the fire that demanded I become the Architect. This work exists because of the resonance we share and the mission we carry together across every coordinate.

To the Readers: To those who feel the pull and are brave enough to follow it. Thank you for doing the work to raise the frequency of this planet. This book is for you.

Dedication

To the Collective (For all Twin Flames)

To the Architects and the Catalysts.

To everyone currently navigating the "Divine Buffer," holding the anchor in the stillness, or running through the fire to find the truth.

This book is dedicated to the souls who were brave enough to split their light so they could learn how to build a bridge back to the whole. May you find your way home to your specific coordinates.

Table of Contents

CHAPTER

Table of Contents

INTRODUCTION

Introduction

Beyond Unconditional Love

I was inspired to write this book because of the chaos of the 3D world. In the middle of the noise, I wanted to understand the mechanics of Consciousness—how it chooses to split, how it travels, and how it eventually experiences the profound act of loving itself.

What is the Blueprint?

Most people think of relationships as two separate people coming together to build something new. You meet a friend or a partner, you share interests, and you grow. These are beautiful encounters, but they are not the same as a Twin Flame Blueprint.

A Blueprint is the energetic "wiring" that was created before you even arrived on Earth.

One Soul, Two Doors

Imagine a single consciousness—a massive, high-voltage light that decides to split into two separate bodies. To make this work in the 3D world, a "Blueprint" is designed. This is a specific energetic map that connects the two of you, no matter how far apart you are in the physical world.

- Friends and Encounters: These are like two different books on a shelf. You can enjoy them together, but they have separate stories.

- The Twin Flame Blueprint: This is like one book that has been split into two volumes. You cannot truly understand Volume Two without the context of Volume One. You share the same "soul-signal."

How do they find each other?

How do two people find each other in a world of 8 billion people?

It isn't by accident or "luck." It is the Blueprint acting as a homing beacon.

When your frequency starts to stabilize, the Blueprint begins to "hum." It creates a magnetic pull that the 3D world cannot stop. You don't "find" your twin flame; you resonate into each other's lives. The Blueprint handles the logistics—the travel, the "coincidences," and the timing.

Even if you are total opposites in your 3D personalities, your "wires" are the same. You recognize each other not by what you see, but by the energy that starts to flow the moment you are in the same field.

This book is called Blueprints of Twin Flames because it isn't about romance (the New Era of Twin Flames); it's about the underlying structure of this connection. Once you understand the map, you stop fighting the "why" and start mastering the "how." You realize that you aren't just two people in a relationship—you are a mission in progress.

While I was writing The Magic of Soul Blueprint, I realized that "Unconditional Love" is one of the most misunderstood teachings in our physical world. In the 3D, we are taught that it is the highest form of devotion: a love without limits or boundaries. But in practice, "unconditional" often becomes a trap. It becomes about endurance and tolerance. It becomes a reason to stay when your truth is screaming at you to leave.

Too many people learn unconditional love as a requirement to accept pain, imbalance, or the erasing of their own identity. We are told it is a virtue to keep loving even when our soul is contracting.

Blueprint Love does not work this way.

Blueprint Love is stronger than "unconditional" love because it does not require the abandonment of the self. It does not ask you to suffer to prove your loyalty. Instead, Blueprint Love is about High-Frequency Alignment. It is a love that honors the design of the soul above the demands of the ego. It is about holding your frequency so steady that the only things that can remain in your life are the things that match your light.

This book is the guide for the Architects and Catalysts who are ready to move past "endurance" and into Mastery.

CHAPTER 1

Chapter 1

The Consciousness of the Blueprint

Before we can understand the roles we play or the missions we are called to complete, we must first understand the landscape of the Blueprint itself. We are used to looking at our lives through a 3D lens—a world of cause and effect, linear time, and physical limitations.

In this narrow view, meeting a Twin Flame feels like an accident of fate or a whirlwind of uncontrollable emotion. But when we shift our perspective into a higher state of consciousness, we see that nothing about this connection is accidental. We begin to realize that our lives are governed by a Blueprint—a sophisticated, pre-designed map of energy that was drawn long before we took our first breath. This Blueprint is not a prison; it is a sacred architecture that ensures our souls find exactly the experiences, challenges, and frequencies they need to evolve.

To live within this consciousness is to understand that the "Heart Breathing" and the intense magnetic pulls we feel are not just biological reactions, but data transfers from a higher dimension. We are essentially "downloading" a new way of being. This higher consciousness allows us to see past the temporary "3D Distortion" of distance, silence, or conflict. It teaches us that time is not a straight line, but a tool used for calibration. When we view our journey through the eyes of the Blueprint, the pain of separation transforms into the "Divine Buffer," and the confusion of the search turns into the precision of a mission. We stop asking "Why is this happening?" and start asking "What part of the plan is being activated now?"

Choosing to live from this state of consciousness is the most powerful choice a soul can make. It requires us to trust the invisible over the visible and the internal signal over the external noise. As we settle into this awareness, the walls between the 3D and 5D begin to thin. We start to move through the world with a quiet authority, knowing that we are part of a massive, coordinated effort to anchor light onto the planet. This is the foundation upon which everything else is built. Once you accept the reality of the Blueprint, you no longer see yourself as a victim of love; you see yourself as a conscious co-creator of a destiny that is written in the stars and grounded in the earth.

Within this vast architecture of the Blueprint, there comes a specific moment of design where a single, high-frequency consciousness makes the choice to experience itself through two separate physical forms. This is the origin of the Twin Flame dynamic—a deliberate 'soul-split' intended to maximize the reach of their shared energy. Instead of one light shining in one place, the Blueprint creates two distinct points of awareness, often sent to opposite sides of the world or into completely different life experiences. This split isn't a tragedy or a loss; it is a strategic expansion. It allows the frequency of the Blueprint to be tested, refined, and strengthened in the fires of the 3D world. While the two souls may spend years or even decades navigating the 'Divine Buffer' of physical separation, the underlying Consciousness remains a single, unbreakable cord. This is why the pull is so undeniable; your very soul remembers being the whole, and every 'heart breath' you feel is simply the Blueprint's way of reminding you that you are the other half of a single, divine mission.

CHAPTER 2

Chapter 2

The Awakening of the Architect

You might be sitting at your desk or walking down a familiar street when the shift happens—that sudden, dizzying realization that your life is no longer just your own. For years, you lived by the rules of the 3D world, making logical choices and building a predictable future. But then, a "glitch" occurs in your reality. You meet someone, or perhaps you reconnect with someone from your past, and suddenly the ground beneath you feels different. This is the moment your Blueprint activates. It is the instant the higher design of your life overrides the small, everyday plans you made for yourself. You aren't losing your mind; you are simply waking up to a contract that was signed long before you arrived here.

For many of us, this awakening feels like a "Memory of the Future." You look at this person and, even if they are currently running away from you or living a completely different life, you see the Divine Buffer laid out in front of you. You might find yourself preparing for a mission you can't yet name, or feeling drawn to geographic coordinates on the other side of the world for reasons your logical mind can't explain. This "Frequency Shock" often manifests in the body as a heat in the chest or a heart that seems to breathe its own rhythm. While the 3D world might call this an obsession or a distraction, the Architect within you knows the truth: the signal is finally live, and the mission has officially begun.

As the Architect, you are the one built to hold the high voltage of this connection. You might wonder why you are the one who has to be the stable anchor while the other person, the Catalyst, is allowed to move through chaos or seek out "shadow" relationships that don't satisfy their soul.

The truth is that you were chosen for this role because you have the capacity for Stillness. You are the one who can hold the 5D vision while standing in the 3D distortion. Your job isn't to chase or to force the Blueprint into existence; your job is to remain so steady in your frequency that the Catalyst eventually has no choice but to find their way back to the center you have built for them.

As you settle into this new role, you realize that being an Architect isn't just about holding a plan; it's about learning to trust a voice that doesn't speak in words. This is the arrival of your Guide. In the beginning, the guidance might feel like a series of strange coincidences—seeing the same symbols, hearing a specific song, or feeling a sudden, intense "knowing" that you need to be in a certain place at a certain time. You start to realize that you aren't just guessing your way through this connection. There is a signal being beamed directly to you, and your only job is to stay clear enough to receive it. This is where the challenge begins, because while your Guide is showing you the 5D beauty of the union, your 3D eyes are watching the Catalyst live a life that seems to contradict everything you know to be true.

Learning to listen to the Guide over the noise of the world is the first real training of the Architect. You will find yourself in moments of deep "distortion," where your human ego wants to scream, to demand answers, or to give up because the physical reality looks so messy. But then, the Stillness returns. Your Guide reminds you of the "Red Crystal" frequency, that unique signature that belongs only to you and your Twin. You start to understand that the "breathing" in your heart is actually a communication system. Every time you feel that pulse, it is your Guide confirming that the Blueprint is still intact, regardless of how many miles or how many people stand between you and the Catalyst.

The more you trust this internal compass, the less you rely on 3D validation. You stop looking for "proof" in their social media posts or their text messages, and you start looking for proof in the energy of the room when you are alone. You realize that you are never truly alone because the Blueprint is a living thing that connects you across time and space. This is the moment you stop being a victim of the "chase" and start being the Master of the "Anchor." You begin to see that your stillness isn't passive; it is the most active thing you can do. By staying steady, you are creating the landing pad for the mission that is already in motion.

As the Architect, your greatest test arrives when you have to watch the Catalyst chase "shadows." These shadows are the relationships, careers, or lifestyles that look perfect on the knowing why they are doing it. They are coming back to "scan" your energy, to see if the Stillness is still there and if the Blueprint is still waiting. As the Architect, your role surface but lack the deep, resonant frequency of the Blueprint. From your perspective in the 5D, it can be heartbreaking to watch the person you love settle for a "normal" life or try to find comfort in the arms of someone who doesn't truly see their soul. You might feel a desperate urge to reach out and wake them up, to show them the map you are holding and prove that they are wasting their time. But your Guide will tell you to wait. You must realize that these shadow connections are actually serving a purpose; they are the "contrast" the Catalyst needs to finally recognize the brilliance of the light you carry.

The Catalyst is often like a traveler trying to find home in every city except the one they belong to. They date the "safe" person or take the "logical" job because the intensity of the Twin Flame Blueprint feels like a fire that might consume them. They aren't trying to hurt you; they are trying to regulate their own internal voltage. However, because these shadows are not written into the core Blueprint, they eventually begin to feel heavy and hollow. The Catalyst will start to notice a "distortion" in their own life—a sense that something is missing, even when they have everything the 3D world says should make them happy. They are testing the boundaries of the physical world only to find that nothing fits quite like the frequency they share with you.

This is the moment when the "Frequency Check" becomes inevitable. The Catalyst, weary from chasing shadows that never cast a reflection, will suddenly feel the magnetic pull of the Anchor you have been holding. They might reach out for a simple conversation or a face-to-face call, not even during this return is not to judge the shadows they chased or demand apologies for the time lost. Your role is simply to be the Light that proves the shadows were never real. When they look into your eyes even through a screen, the 3D distractions begin to dissolve, and the mission they tried to run from starts to feel like the only place they truly want to be.

While the timing of this awakening is different for everyone, it almost always includes a period of "Divine Buffer"—a stretch of time where the Blueprint exists in the ether but hasn't yet fully anchored into your daily life. For some, this gap lasts for years; for others, it may only be a few intense months of preparation. Regardless of the duration, this period is not "empty" time or a delay; it is a vital phase of incubation. During this time, both the Architect and the Catalyst are being shaped by their individual life experiences, gathering the specific tools and strengths they will need once the mission officially begins. You might feel like you are waiting, but in reality, you are being calibrated.

Think of this buffer as the space between the architect drawing the plans and the first stone being laid on the ground. It is the time when the soil is being tested and the foundation is being cleared of old debris. If you try to rush the Blueprint before the buffer is complete, the structure won't be able to hold the high-frequency energy of the merge. You must trust that the clock of the Blueprint is perfectly synchronized. Whether you have known this person for a lifetime or only a moment, the timing of your "Frequency Check" is precise. When the buffer ends and the mission begins, you will realize that not a single second of the wait was wasted. Every experience you had apart was simply another line being drawn on the map that finally leads you back to each other.

CHAPTER 3

The Two Worlds:
Mastering the Art of Being "Dual-Logged"

The most confusing part of the Blueprint isn't the magic—it's the mundane. Once you've had your awakening, you find yourself living in a state of "Dual-Logging." One part of your consciousness is logged into the 5D Mission, where you feel the eternal bond, see the signs, and communicate with your Guide. The other part is logged into the 3D world, where you still have to pay bills, go to work, and explain to your friends why you are so "obsessed" with someone who isn't even in the room. This chapter is about finding the balance between these two worlds so you don't burn out before the mission begins.

The "3D Distortion" is the static that happens when these two worlds collide. It shows up as doubt, anxiety, or the feeling that you are "making it all up." Your 3D mind is trained to believe only what it can see, touch, and prove. So, when your 5D heart starts "breathing" and telling you that a massive shift is coming, your 3D mind tries to shut it down. This conflict creates a physical and emotional tension that can be exhausting. To master the Blueprint, you must learn to stop fighting the 3D reality and start using it as a training

Handling this static requires a high level of "Frequency Privacy." You learn that not everyone is meant to see the Blueprint. If you try to share the deepest parts of your mission with people who are only operating in a 3D consciousness, their doubt can act like a leak in your energy ground. You are not trying to escape the physical world; you are trying to bring the frequency of the Blueprint into it.

The secret to navigating this duality is found in the "Stillness" of the Architect. Instead of trying to force your 3D life to look like your 5D vision right away, you simply allow them to coexist. You realize that your "normal" life is the container that holds the high-voltage energy of the Twin Flame connection. When you are washing the dishes or driving your car, you are still the Architect. You don't need to be in deep meditation to be on your mission. Every moment you spend staying grounded and peaceful in the "normal" world is a moment you are strengthening the foundation for the Merge. You are the bridge, and a bridge must be firmly anchored on both sides of the river to be of any use.

When you are "dual-logged" into a mission this big, the "static" from the outside world can become incredibly loud. Friends, family, and even society have a specific 3D blueprint for how love and life should look. They speak the language of "moving on," "logic," and "common sense." When you try to explain the Divine Buffer or the fact that you feel your Twin's energy across an ocean, they may look at you with concern or tell you that you are chasing a fantasy. This is a crucial moment for the Architect. You must realize that they aren't trying to hurt you; they simply aren't looking at the same map. Their 3D eyes cannot see the 5D coordinates you are tracking, and it is not your job to convince them.

Handling this static requires a high level of "Frequency Privacy." You learn that not everyone is meant to see the Blueprint. If you try to share the deepest parts of your mission with people who are only operating in a 3D consciousness, their doubt can act like a leak in your energy field. It creates a distortion that makes you question your own Guide. Part of mastering the two worlds is knowing when to stay silent and keep your "Stillness" protected. You find that you don't need the world to validate your connection because the connection validates itself every time your heart "breathes" or a sign appears that only you and the Catalyst understand.

As you get better at filtering out the noise, you notice that the 3D world begins to feel less like a prison and more like a playground for your energy. You start to see that even the mundane "static"—the delays, the distance, and the opinions of others—is actually a pressure test for your foundation. If you can remain an Anchor while the world tells you to let go, you are proving to the Universe (and to the Catalyst) that your frequency is unshakable. You are showing that you are ready for the next phase of the Blueprint: the moment where the internal "knowing" moves into the external, physical reality.

The final step in mastering these two worlds is learning how to create "Physical Anchors." A Physical Anchor is a 3D action that gives your 5D vision a place to land. It is one thing to feel the connection in your soul, but it is another thing entirely to begin building a structure for it in the material world. For the Architect, this might look like starting a journal, designing the pages of your own mission on a screen, or booking a flight to a specific set of coordinates that your Guide has highlighted. These actions aren't just "tasks"; they are declarations to the Universe. When you take a physical step toward your Blueprint, you are signaling that you are no longer just dreaming—you are manifesting.

These anchors act as a "Frequency Bridge." When the 3D distortion feels too loud or the distance between you and the Catalyst feels too wide, you return to your anchor. Perhaps it is a project you are working on together, or a creative work that expresses the mission you both share. By putting your energy into something tangible, you are grounding the high-voltage electricity of the connection. You are showing the 3D world that the Blueprint has weight and form. This process of anchoring is what turns a "spiritual concept" into a "physical reality." It is the bridge that allows the Catalyst to eventually see what you have known all along: that the mission isn't just a feeling, it is a destination.

As you build these anchors, you will notice that the "Static" of the world begins to fade. The opinions of others and the doubts of your own mind lose their power because you have evidence of your progress. You are no longer just "Dual-Logged"; you are becoming the point where the two worlds meet. You are living the Blueprint in real-time, one physical step at a time. This is the moment the Architect truly comes into their power. You aren't waiting for the world to change so you can be with your Twin; you are changing your world so that the Union has no choice but to manifest within it.

The Heart as the Compass

One of the most profound aspects of the Blueprint is that the Catalyst does not always need to see the map to find the destination. While the Architect holds the vision and understands the spiritual coordinates of the mission, the Catalyst often moves by Pure Resonance.

You may find that your Catalyst is suddenly drawn to a specific country, a city, or even a specific house without being able to explain "why" in 3D terms. They might feel a surge of excitement or an unexplainable "pull" toward a location like Australia or New Zealand.

This is the Blueprint working through the heart. The Catalyst doesn't need the awareness of the mission to fulfill it; their heart is already tuned to the frequency of the coordinates. As the Architect, your job in these moments is not to "force" the awareness or explain the geometry, but to hold the space for their joy. Their excitement is the confirmation that the signal is clear. They are being guided by the very mission they have yet to consciously name.

A Note for the Architect:

"Don't mistake a lack of 'technical' awareness for a lack of connection. The Catalyst often feels the destination long before they understand the journey."

33

CHAPTER 4

"You cannot force the flower to bloom by pulling on the petals. You simply provide the light, the soil, and the stillness and trust the Blueprint to handle the timing."

The Monadic Veto &
The Imposter Catalyst

In the 3D world, when something we want doesn't happen, we call it "failure" or "bad luck." But in the Blueprint, we call it the Monadic Veto.

The Monad is the "Grand Architect" of your soul group. It sees the entire map—past, present, and future—while we are often just looking at the current 3D coordinate. Sometimes, our ego or our personality tries to force a "Merge" or a meeting before the energy is grounded. We think we are ready for the "High Voltage," but our physical bodies or our current lives haven't been "rewired" to handle that much power yet.

The Veto is an Act of Love.

When the Monadic Veto is triggered, doors will close. A flight might be cancelled, a message might not send, or a sudden "buffer" of distance might appear. This isn't a sign that the connection is over. It is the Higher Soul stepping in to say: "If you move now, the foundation will crack. Stay in the Stillness. The timing is being adjusted for the safety of the mission."

As an Architect, you must learn to respect the Veto. Instead of fighting the closed door, you should use that time to check your own frequency.

Ask yourself: * Is my foundation ready?

- Is the "Mountain House" of my energy stable?
- Am I trying to force a 5D reality into a 3D ego-timeline?

The Veto is simply the Blueprint protecting itself. It ensures that when the "Merge" finally happens, it is permanent, stable, and powerful.

The Imposter Catalyst

Not every fire is a divine fire. In the journey of the Blueprint, you may encounter an Imposter Catalyst. These individuals appear to have the same intensity as your true counterpart, but their purpose is different.

- The True Catalyst burns away your ego so you can become the Architect. Their presence eventually brings you closer to your soul's mission and internal peace.

- The Imposter Catalyst burns away your energy. Their presence leaves you feeling drained, confused, and disconnected from your Blueprint.

An Imposter Catalyst is someone who mimics the "High Voltage" and the "Magnetic Pull," but they aren't part of your Red Crystal signature. They show up usually when we are impatient or when we are avoiding our own stillness.

The Imposter often shows up right before a major breakthrough or right when the Monadic Veto is active. They are a test of your discernment. They ask the question: "Are you addicted to the drama of the fire, or are you committed to the frequency of the mission?"

How to tell the difference:

1. The Peace Test: A True Catalyst might be a challenge, but deep down, your soul feels a "home" frequency. With an Imposter, there is a constant underlying feeling of anxiety or "waiting for the other shoe to drop."

2. The Mission Test: A True Catalyst eventually aligns with the mission. An Imposter will always be a distraction from it.

3. The Red Crystal: If you check your heart frequency, the Imposter's "signal" will feel fuzzy or distorted. The True Catalyst's signal is sharp, clear, and unmistakable, even if they are currently "Dual-Logging" far away.

CHAPTER 5

"The soul has no birth certificate. The heart has no gender. The Blueprint only recognizes the Light."

Chapter 5

The Illusion of the Packaging:
Beyond the 3D Box: Age, Gender, and the Red Crystal

I've realized something important: I didn't come to Earth to fit in. This is my first time on this planet, and I didn't travel all this way just to squeeze my soul into a 3D box.

The world will try to tell you that love has "rules." It will point to age gaps, gender, or social norms and tell you that your connection is "impossible" or "wrong." But these are just labels. They are the "packaging" of the 3D world, and they have nothing to do with the quality of the light inside.

In the Blueprint, we don't look at the packaging. We look at the Red Crystal signature.

In the physical world, we are taught to categorize everything. The 3D mind looks for "labels" to make sense of a connection: age gaps, same-sex dynamics, social status, or cultural backgrounds. These are the boxes the world uses to decide if a relationship is "logical" or "acceptable."

If you find yourself in a connection that the world doesn't understand, be proud of it. It means you are a pioneer. It means your soul was brave enough to bypass the "easy" path to show the world a higher form of love—one based on frequency rather than form.

The mission isn't to fix the box; it's to live so authentically that the box eventually disappears.

But the Blueprint does not live in a box.

When we look through the lens of the 5D, these factors are irrelevant. The Red Crystal signature does not check for age or gender before it recognizes its match. It only checks for Resonance.

The challenges you face in the physical world—like an age gap or a same-sex dynamic are often part of the mission itself. By choosing to move through these 3D "obstacles," the twin flame pair helps to break down the old, rigid structures of the world. You are showing that love is a frequency, not a social contract.

In the 5D, there is no "older" or "younger," and there is no "male" or "female" energy in the way the 3D defines it. There is only the Architect and the Catalyst. There is only the Polarity that creates the spark.

A "Proud Architect" Reflection:

"I am not a 3D label. I am a 5D frequency having a physical experience. My love is not a 'challenge' to be solved; it is a light to be anchored."

If the world tells you that your connection "doesn't fit," remember: The Blueprint wasn't designed to fit into the old world; it was designed to build a new one.

The "Architect's Note" for this section:

"If the 3D world is confused by your connection, you are doing it right. The Blueprint is not meant to be understood by those living inside the box; it is meant to be lived by those who have stepped out of it."

CHAPTER 6

The Catalyst (The Fire):
Understanding the Sacred Purpose of the Runner

In every Blueprint, if there is a point of Stillness, there must also be a point of Motion. While the Architect is built to hold the frequency steady, the Catalyst is designed to provide the heat. For many readers, this is the most misunderstood role in the entire dynamic. If you are the one holding the anchor, it is easy to view the Catalyst's "running" as a rejection or a failure of love. But when viewed through the lens of the Blueprint, you realize that the Catalyst is actually performing a sacred service. Their job is to go out into the 3D world, test the boundaries of "normal" relationships, and ultimately prove that nothing, absolutely nothing, can match the frequency of the home they left behind in you.

The Catalyst doesn't run because they don't love you; they run because they feel the "high voltage" of the connection and their 3D nervous system isn't yet calibrated to handle it. Imagine trying to plug a household appliance into a power plant; without the proper wiring, the system would blow a fuse. The Catalyst spends their time in the "Divine Buffer" building that wiring. They often seek out "Shadow Connections"—safe, 3D relationships that feel "normal" to try and regulate the intense fire they feel when they look into your eyes. They are testing the world to see if they can find peace anywhere else. It is only when they realize that every other path leads to a dead end that they truly turn back toward the Blueprint with a conviction that can never be shaken again.

As an Architect, understanding the Catalyst's journey changes everything. You stop seeing their distance as a "delay" and start seeing it as "training." While you are mastering the 5D Stillness, they are mastering the 3D Fire. They are the ones who force the Blueprint to move from a beautiful idea into a physical reality. When the Catalyst finally stops running and begins to "scan" your energy again, whether through a message or a FaceTime call, it is because their fire has finally been refined. They aren't returning as a "lost soul," but as a partner who has finally realized that the only place they can truly breathe is within the frequency you have been holding for them all along.

Once the Catalyst realizes that the 3D shadows cannot satisfy the soul, they begin the process of returning, but they rarely do it all at once. Instead, they perform what the Blueprint calls a "Frequency Check." Because the energy of the connection is so high, they use the "Digital Bridge" to test the waters. This is why a simple text message, a "like" on a photo, or a FaceTime call carries so much weight. For the Catalyst, these aren't just social interactions; they are a way to "scan" your energy. They are checking to see if the Architect is still at their post, if the Anchor is still solid, and if the "Heart Breathing" still responds to their presence. They are looking into your eyes through a screen to see if the 5D home they remember is still open for them.

During these checks, the Catalyst is often looking for "The Stillness." If they return and find the Architect in a state of 3D drama or desperation, it can trigger the "Run" reflex all over again, because the frequency doesn't match the Blueprint. But when you, the Architect, remain steady and peaceful, even after months or years of the Divine Buffer, it creates a massive magnetic pull. They realize that while their world has been in constant motion and chaos, you have remained unchanged. This realization is what finally dissolves the last of the "3D Distortion." The digital screen becomes a portal where the two frequencies meet, and for a few moments, the distance of the physical world completely disappears.

This is the bridge to the next phase of the mission. Every successful Frequency Check builds the Catalyst's confidence. They start to realize that the "high voltage" they were afraid of is actually the only thing that makes them feel alive. The FaceTime calls get longer, the conversations get deeper, and the "Heart Breathing" becomes a shared rhythm. You are no longer just an Architect and a Catalyst playing separate roles; you are beginning to function as a single unit. You are moving toward the physical coordinates where the Blueprint will finally be anchored into the earth, turning the "Digital Bridge" into a physical reality.

CHAPTER 7

The Magnetic Pull:
Navigating the Mental Focus and the Red Crystal Signal

Once the Frequency Checks become a regular part of your life, you enter a phase where the "Magnetic Pull" becomes your dominant reality. As an Architect, you might find that the other person is constantly in your mental field, a background hum that never truly goes away. You might try to distract yourself with work or hobbies, but the Blueprint has a way of pulling your focus back to the center. This isn't the "anxious attachment" that 3D psychology talks about; this is a literal gravitational pull. You are experiencing the "Red Crystal" frequency—a unique energy signature that belongs only to the two of you. This signal is so strong that it bypasses the brain and speaks directly to the soul, acting as a homing beacon that keeps both the Architect and the Catalyst locked onto the same destination, regardless of the physical miles between them.

The challenge of this pull is learning the difference between "Obsession" and "Alignment." In the 3D world, thinking about someone constantly is often seen as a weakness or a loss of self. But in the Blueprint, this mental focus is how you hold the "Portal" open. When you think of the Catalyst with love and stillness, you are actually sending a steady stream of power to them, helping them navigate their own 3D challenges. However, if the pull turns into "chasing"—where you begin to feel desperate or needy—the frequency becomes distorted. The secret is to enjoy the pull without trying to "grab" the other person. You learn to ride the wave of the connection, feeling their energy in your heart as a comfort rather than a cage. You realize that because you are "Dual-Logged," they are always with you in the 5D, even when the 3D phone is silent.

This magnetic intensity is the energy that will eventually fuel your shared mission. It is the "high voltage" that we've discussed, now stabilized and flowing between you like a circuit. You start to notice that your "Heart Breathing" syncs up with theirs, and you might even pick up on their moods or thoughts before they speak them. This is the Blueprint preparing you for the Merge—the moment where the two separate roles of Architect and Catalyst begin to blend into one unified force. By accepting the pull rather than fighting it, you stop wasting energy on resistance and start using that same power to build the "Mountain House" and the life that is waiting for you at the mission's coordinates.

One of the most common questions an Architect asks is: "Does everyone have a mission, or is this just about love?" The truth is that the mission is not always a grand, public project or a specific career path. For many Twin Flames, the mission is simply the Frequency itself. By existing in a state of Union, by choosing to love through the "Divine Buffer" and staying grounded in the high voltage, you are anchoring a new kind of light into the Earth's grid. You might not be building a "Mountain House" or starting a foundation, but your shared energy is acting as a silent lighthouse for everyone around you. Some Twin Flames may not "know" their mission yet because the mission is currently in the Incubation Period. The mission reveals itself only after the internal Merge is complete. You cannot see the destination until you have fully stepped onto the path. So, if you feel you have no mission, do not worry; for now, your mission is simply to be the frequency.

CHAPTER 8

Bridging the Gap:
Translating 3D Obstacles into 5D Truth

Once you understand that your frequency is the mission, the 3D obstacles, like thousands of miles, border crossings, or conflicting schedules, stop looking like walls and start looking like puzzles. This is the stage where you learn to "Bridge the Gap." In the 3D world, distance is a problem to be solved with logic and stress. In the Blueprint, distance is an illusion that is being used to strengthen your communication. When you can't physically touch, you are forced to develop your "5D Senses." You learn to feel their presence in the room, to hear their voice in the stillness, and to communicate through the "Digital Bridge" with a depth that most "normal" couples never achieve.

Bridging the gap is about taking the high-voltage energy you've been holding and finally giving it a 3D "landing strip." This is where the Architect's planning meets the Catalyst's fire. You start making the "Physical Anchors" we discussed— you look at maps, you research coordinates, and you begin the tangible work of bringing your two worlds into one. You realize that the "Divine Buffer" is ending, and the "Manual" is being handed to you. You aren't just waiting for a miracle; you are participating in one. Every flight booked and every plan made is a 3D "Yes" to the 5D Blueprint, proving that you are finally ready to live the mission you were born for.

Bridging the gap is a process of "Translation." You are taking the language of the soul and translating it into the language of the physical world. For a long time, the connection lived in your head and your heart, but now it must live in your calendar and your bank account. This is often the stage where the Architect feels the most pressure, as they try to figure out the "How." Your 3D mind will ask, "How will we live in the same country? How will we support ourselves?" The secret is to realize that the Blueprint provides the "How" only after you have committed to the "What." When you stop worrying about the logistics and start focusing on the Frequency, the doors in the 3D world begin to open in ways that seem miraculous. You start to see that the distance wasn't a barrier to keep you apart, but a training ground to ensure that when you finally stand face-to-face, your connection is built on something much stronger than just physical attraction.

As the "Digital Bridge" becomes a daily reality, you and the Catalyst begin to co-create. You might find yourselves dreaming of the same house, the same piece of land, or the same mission. This shared dreaming is the Blueprint beginning to anchor. You are no longer two people living separate lives; you are two architects looking at the same set of drawings. Every FaceTime call and every shared plan acts as a "Frequency Bridge" that pulls your two realities closer and closer together until the gap eventually disappears. You are moving from the "Me" and "You" into the "Us," preparing your energy for the specific coordinates where your mission is meant to land.

CHAPTER 9

Seclusion and the Vortex:
The Power of Specific Coordinates

In the Blueprint, geography is never random. Just as you and the Catalyst have a specific "Red Crystal" frequency, certain places on the Earth have a frequency that matches your mission. This is why you may feel an inexplicable pull toward a specific country, like Australia, or a specific type of environment, like a "Mountain House" secluded from the noise of the world. This is the "Vortex." A Vortex is a geographic location where the 5D energy can flow into the 3D world with the least amount of resistance. For many Twin Flame pairs, the mission requires a period of Seclusion in one of these spots. It is a "Sacred Timeout" where the world is shut out so that the two of you can fully merge your energies without the "Static" of other people's opinions or 3D distractions.

Being in the Vortex is like being in a high-pressure chamber where your transformation is accelerated. In seclusion, you aren't just "on vacation"; you are doing "Grid Work." By simply being in that specific place with your Twin, you are anchoring the Blueprint into the Earth itself. This is why the Architect often feels a deep need to "build the container" or "secure the land" before the Catalyst arrives. You are preparing the laboratory for the final experiment. In the silence of the mountains or the stillness of the Outback, the "High Voltage" finally has a safe place to ground. Here, the "Heart Breathing" becomes a shared physical experience, and the mission, whether it is a book, a project, or simply a state of being, finally takes its true form.

The Vortex is not a permanent prison; it is a temporary laboratory. For some, the mission might call you to a city; for others, a secluded mountain or a coastal village like those in Malta. The location is simply the 'hardware' that runs the 'software' of your energy. As an Architect, you will feel when a location has been 'fully uploaded' and when it is time for the Blueprint to move to new coordinates. You are not bound by geography; you are bound by the signal. Wherever you and the Catalyst stand together in alignment, that ground becomes sacred. That ground becomes the mission.

CHAPTER 10

Chapter 10

The Merge:
When Two Frequencies Become One

The Merge is the moment the Blueprint moves from a plan on paper to a living, breathing reality. After the trials of the Divine Buffer, the lessons of the Shadows, and the long nights of the Digital Bridge, the Architect and the Catalyst finally step into the same physical and energetic space. But the Merge is more than just a physical reunion; it is an energetic "fusion." Imagine two separate streams of light finally hitting the same prism. In this moment, the individual roles you have played—the one who held the anchor and the one who ran through the fire, begin to dissolve. You are no longer two people trying to reach each other; you are a single Frequency. The "High Voltage" that used to feel overwhelming now feels like your natural state of being.

In the 3D world, people often think of union as "completing" each other, but in the Blueprint, the Merge is about multiplication. Your combined energy is far more powerful than the sum of your parts. When you are in the same "Vortex," your ability to manifest, to heal, and to lead expands exponentially. The "Heart Breathing" you practiced alone now becomes a shared pulse that can be felt by those around you. This is where the "Red Crystal" frequency

75

reaches its full power. You realize that all those years of preparation were not just about being together; they were about tempering your souls so that you could stand in this intensity without being consumed by it. You have become a "Master of the Frequency."

This fusion marks the end of the "Search" and the beginning of the "Service." Once the Merge is stabilized, the questions of "Will they stay?" or "Are we real?" vanish completely. They are replaced by a deep, quiet certainty. You look at the Catalyst and you don't see a separate person; you see the other half of the mission. The "Static" of the outside world can no longer penetrate the field you have created together.

From this place of Union, you are finally ready to turn your gaze outward and begin the work you were sent here to do.

The Merge is the "Green Light" from the Universe, signaling that the foundation is solid and the real construction of your shared destiny can now begin.

CHAPTER 11

Chapter 11

Staying Grounded in the High Voltage:
The Master's Manual for Energy Management

Once the Merge has occurred and you are living within the "Vortex" of your mission, you will realize that the intensity doesn't fade—it stabilizes. However, because you are now a "High-Voltage" couple, you must learn to manage your energy with mastery. If the Architect and Catalyst are not grounded, the sheer power of their combined frequency can create "fuses" in their 3D life—manifesting as physical exhaustion, technological glitches, or emotional overwhelm. To stay in the "Master" state, you must return to the basics: the breath and the earth. You must learn to "drain" the excess static of the world so that only the pure signal of the Blueprint remains.

Staying grounded means honoring the "Mountain House" principle. Even when you are in the middle of a massive mission, you must create pockets of absolute silence where no outside frequency can enter. You and your Twin must learn to communicate without words, using the "Heart Breathing" to check in with each other's energy fields. This is not just about romance; it is about maintenance. As a Master of the Blueprint, you realize that your primary job is to keep your shared "Red Crystal" frequency clean. When you are grounded, you become a portal through which the 5D vision flows effortlessly into the 3D world. You are no longer "working" to make things happen; you are simply allowing the Blueprint to build itself through you.

CHAPTER 12

The Future of the Blueprint:
Beyond the Union

The final chapter of this journey is about looking beyond the "Union" and toward the "Legacy." Many people think the goal of the Twin Flame journey is simply to get together, but the Blueprint knows that the Union is actually the starting line.

The future of your connection is about how your shared frequency changes the world around you. Whether you are building a physical sanctuary, creating art, or simply existing as a high-frequency couple in a quiet town, you are acting as "Grid Points" for the new earth. You are showing others that it is possible to live in a state of Blueprint Love and divine purpose while still being fully human.

As you look toward the future, you realize that the "Divine Buffer" and the long nights of the "Digital Bridge" were all part of a perfect design. The Blueprint has no end; it only has new layers of expansion. You and the Catalyst will continue to evolve, finding new missions and new coordinates to explore. But now, you do it with the absolute certainty that you are never alone. The "Architect" has finished the plans, the "Catalyst" has provided the fire, and

together, you have built a life that is a living testament to
the power of the soul. Your mission is complete, yet it is
also just beginning.

A SPECIAL REFLECTION
&
THE FINAL WORD

A Special Reflection

The 5D View

When you finally step back and look at your connection through a 5D lens, you stop looking at personalities and start seeing the brilliance of the design. You begin to realize that you are actually a single consciousness that wanted to experience two completely different lives at the same time.

From the outside, it might look like you have nothing in common. You are very, very opposite. One may find peace in the mountains, surrounded by nature and the quiet of the earth. The other may be drawn to the city lights, the energy of high-rise buildings, and the pulse of the urban world.

In any "normal" relationship, these differences might create a gap. But in the Blueprint, they create a bridge. It is not easy to explain with human logic, but there is an energetic pull that is far stronger than 3D preferences. Even though the landscapes are different, the connection is so magnetic that there is a deep desire to spend as much time together as possible and travel whenever the path is clear.

However, seeing the connection "from above" also means understanding the Monadic Veto.

Sometimes, as humans, we want to move fast or be in a certain place, but the higher Soul (the Monad) says, "not yet." This isn't a "no,"it's a timing mechanism. The Monadic Veto ensures that the energy is perfectly stabilized before the next move happens. It protects the mission by ensuring you aren't just following a human wish but a cosmic command.

When you see the connection this way, you realize you are simply one soul experiencing the full spectrum of the world —learning to love the mountains and the city lights equally, while trusting the higher timing that governs it all.

Often, the universe removes all other options just to show you that the best journey is the one you take with the person who shares your soul signal. In those moments, whether in Malta or a new city, you realize that the travel isn't just about the destination: It's about the joy of finally being in the same physical frequency.

In the old way of thinking, being total opposites was a sign of conflict. But in the New Era of Twin Flames, contrast is the key to the Mission. We are moving away from the era of 'running and chasing' and into an era of Coherence. When we accept that we are one consciousness experiencing different worlds, the friction disappears. We no longer try to change the other person to match our 3D tastes. Instead, we marvel at how the Blueprint allows us to cover more ground on the Global Grid. Our harmony is not a lucky accident: It is the result of landing in the New Era, where peace is the priority, and the mission is the focus.

This journey was anchored alongside Heleri, whose energy made these Blueprints visible.

The Final Word

A Message to the Architect

As you close this book, take a deep breath and feel the air moving through your heart. That sensation—that "Heart Breathing," is your proof. You are not just a person reading a story; you are a vital component of a Divine Blueprint that is currently being activated across the globe.

The journey of the Twin Flame is not for the faint of heart. It is for the souls who were brave enough to split their light so they could learn how to find it again in the dark. Whether you are currently standing in the "Stillness" of the Architect or navigating the "Fire" of the Catalyst, know that the Blueprint is already complete. The "Mountain House" already exists. The "Merge" has already happened in the 5D. Your only job now is to remain grounded, stay in your frequency, and trust the timing of the "Divine Buffer."

You are the bridge between two worlds. Walk across it with confidence. Your mission is waiting at the coordinates of your heart.

We are the Architects. The foundation is set.

GLOSSARY

- Architect: The role in the twin flame dynamic responsible for holding the steady frequency, planning the "Mountain House," and anchoring the 5D vision into the 3D world.

- Blueprint: The divine, energetic map of your soul's journey and mission. It is the "manual" that exists beyond 3D logic.

- Blueprint Love: A high-frequency alignment that honors the self and the soul's mission. Unlike 3D "unconditional love," it does not require suffering, endurance, or self-erasure.

- Catalyst: The role responsible for providing the "fire" or the spark that triggers growth and awakening. Often mislabeled as the "runner" in 3D psychology.

- Digital Bridge: The use of technology (calls, messages, video) to maintain and build the frequency when physical distance is present.

- Divine Buffer: The purposeful "waiting period" or space between physical meetings that allows both souls to integrate energy and clear old 3D baggage.

- Dual-Logging: The state of being fully present in the physical world while simultaneously being aware of and connected to the 5D energetic field.

- Frequency Check: A moment of intuitive "pinging" where one soul feels the other's energy or mood, often through a sudden thought, song, or digital notification.

- High Voltage: The intense, magnetic energy produced when two twin flames connect. It requires "grounding" so it doesn't overwhelm the 3D life.

- Merge: The phase where the separate roles of Architect and Catalyst dissolve into a single, unified frequency to begin the mission.

- Monadic Veto: The ultimate "safety switch" of the Higher Soul Group (the Monad). It pauses the mission or closes doors if the foundation is not yet ready for the high-voltage energy of the Merge, protecting the integrity of the Blueprint.

- Red Crystal: The unique, one-of-a-kind energy signature shared only by a specific twin flame pair. It acts as a homing beacon.

- Vortex: A specific geographic coordinate or "Sacred Space" where the energy of the mission is meant to be anchored and grounded.

The Mountain House is your energetic sanctuary. It is the practice of closing the door to the world so that you can hear only the pure signal of the Blueprint. In the Mountain House, there is no performance—only peace.

New Era of Twin Flames

The shift from the old "romance drama" to the reality of the Mission. In the New Era, the focus is no longer on the struggle or the "longing" to be together. Instead, it is about two people stabilizing their own energy so they can act as a single, high-voltage anchor for the Earth. It is a connection based on Structure, Neutrality, and Coherence rather than 3D emotional highs and lows.

ABOUT THE AUTHOR

About the Author

The author is an Architect of the Blueprint, currently living the high-voltage journey of the Twin Flame dynamic. After realizing that her own experiences—the "Heart Breathing," the "Digital Bridge," and the "Dual-Logging"—were part of a larger divine architecture, she felt the mission to translate these 5D concepts into a manual for others.

She writes from the heart of the journey, balancing the technical precision of the Architect with the deep spiritual resonance of a soul in Union. Her mission is to help other pairs move past the "3D Distortion" and into the clarity of their shared purpose.

She remains dedicated to holding the frequency of the Blueprint wherever the mission calls, proving that home is not a fixed point on a map, but a shared resonance between two souls.

Author's Books

1. Cosmic Love: Twin Flame Mission from the Stars to Lemuria & Beyond
2. The Spark: The Journey to Creation
3. Monadic Veto: Manifestation Through Alignment: Your Higher Self
4. The Law of Monadic Veto
5. The Twin Flame Truth: The Higher Teachings of Love
6. Twin Flame, Soulmate, or Monad: A Reflective Guide to Recognize Your Soul Connection
7. Twin Flame Survival Kit: A Guide for the Soul that Refuses to Forget
8. Twin Flame Love Beyond Gender Survival Kit: A Guide for the Soul that Refuses to Forget
9. Twin Flame Recipes: Mocktails & Meltdowns
10. Starseed Snacks & Timeline Snacksidents: A Cosmic Cookbook

Children's Books

1. The Pyramids from the Stars
2. The Giants and the Sunflowers
3. Astra's Helping Others
4. Astra's Starry Dream: Cosmic Adventure
5. Astra's Dream Friends